The Imagination of a Stressed Teenager

A BOOK OF POEMS

Evrin Galindo

2020

Book cover design by Evrin A. Galindo

www.worksbyevrin.com

Amazon eBook ASIN: B08G3GFW3F
Paperback ISBN: 978-0-578-84739-9

Contents

Introduction

The poems in this book were written throughout my teenage years. You will see how my emotions began to change from ages 12 to 18. These poems portray many emotions, and I hope they help readers connect to their feelings. Also, to any parents who have children going through a rough time, I hope this will help you understand what your children might be feeling. I hope you enjoy this book.

Again and Again

I don't need a mirror, I can barely see you, but I remember.

A doppelgänger, another stranger, remake the danger.

I barely stood for it, took it for granted, my guilty pleasure.

Again and again. Here we go. Time to start from the heart.

Others need to be the same way, but I got to be the unlucky fool today.

You don't know what goes through my head.

I send you a text when I know that you're on. I get a little chill when you look at your phone.

How can I tell if that smile is sweet? Should I give one back, or should I leave?

I know it's dumb and annoying; no one gets it.

Again and again, I just don't want to go back.

Forget, Forgot

It's like I mirror you.
It's my curse to be like you.

It's really hard to be like someone you hate.
It's excessive to always spectate.

I just can't get over the pain.
I'm tired of always feeling the same.

I hate you, I hate you not.
I wish I could say I forgot.

You haven't seen anything yet.
In the end, it will be you who wants to forget.

Trapped

Why do we think like this?
We live our happy lives, but imagine hell in our minds.

We feed off of pleasure and bliss.
But in our minds we become addicted, completely tied.

Always smiling, and laughing too.
Always thinking of torment and pain.

Why do we think of the things we lose?
We never really stay the same.

We are free to roam and live our lives.
But we imagine we are trapped, completely caged.

Why is it that we daydream we die?
We pretend that everything will fade.

Do we like it, do we want to be kept?
Do we want to be slaves, all for sorrow?

No matter how much we've slept we can't escape
tomorrow.

Why do we imagine we are trapped?
In reality, we are free.

I'm guessing that something snapped.
Now we all belong to thee.

Puzzled

Pieces put together, then taken apart.

Edges glued together, then painted dark.

Tiny pictures make a portrait.

Smiling faces on skin that's porcelain.

A game design to challenge us all.

A brain teaser, that is all.

Mix matched, swapped, and scrambled.

Fixed, attached, popped, and dabbled.

Our so-called perfect us, in a game that struggles.

So smile with trust, don't look so puzzled.

Wounds

I took a bullet at age twelve.
I didn't recover so well.

I got stabbed when I was thirteen.
I tried to hide the bleeding.

I got crushed while at fourteen.
Everything became unsporting.

I took a wound for the fourth time.
My heart holds these scars of mine.

They say my past is nothing of concern.
But they don't understand how much it burned.

Behind my smile I'm hiding pain.
It takes someone to drive another insane.

Open my wounds and make them sore.
It's better, anyway, to not care anymore.

I'm cutting off all chances and stopping the dreams.
There are no more dances, and no more me.

I'm done being last, the nice one is in the past.

If you think I'm bad then watch me go rotten.

Forget what you had, because I have already forgotten.

These wounds are what make me the way that I am.
If you don't like it, well I don't give a damn.

I'm sorry if you thought wrong. It's not me who isn't strong.

To all who wounded me thank you for my past.
Now I have a journey and I will make it last.

Door

They keep opening the door, my head just aches.

They keep asking me for more, all I feel is pain.

No more suffering, a whole new life in buffering.

But they keep opening the door.

My friend keeps saying things are better but the future seems so farther.

Keep on changing my new pace, forget that old ugly face.

And they keep opening the door.

The night only gets darker, my breathing keeps on getting harder.

I threw away all the evil, now I can start a new level.

Forget about me, you are the last thing I need.

So no, I won't open the door.

Me

I just want you to go away.
Disappear, vanish, fall in shame.

You killed my pride, you made me hurt.
You always tried to play nice? Ha, yeah sure.

I fell hard, you used my trust.
But now is now, and I haven't lost.

This is me and I won't change for you.
I don't care about the things you do.

The things you said won't stay in my head.
I'll be happy until my death.

This is me and I won't change for you.

I can't stop the memories.
The time you made it feel like it was me.

You made me cry, you stole my joy.
I felt like a useless toy.

I felt love, I gave you trust.
But now is now, and I haven't lost.

This is me and I won't change for you.

I don't care about the things you do.

The things you said won't stay in my head.
I'll be happy until death.

This is me and I won't change for you.

Now I'm a whole new kind.
Still full of joy, a peace of mind.

Go ahead hold onto your gift.
The last thing from me you'll ever get.

In fact, you can ignore me all you want, because I don't care that much.

This is me and I won't change for you.

My Head

There's a memory playing in my head.
Part of me wants you dead.

You hurt my heart, you hurt me bad.
I felt like I died, you made me sad.

I gave you gifts to show my trust.
You took it for granted and made me crush.

I want to forget you, I don't love you.

You mean nothing.
You are not something.

Just leave my life, you're not part of me anymore.

Goodbye

Bye

I guess I should say bye.
I honestly don't know if I will cry.

Was that a straight face, or did you stay in the same place?

Why can't you leave my head?
You make my heart and mind feel dead.

Why can't I forget it, forget the past?
So I regret it, do I fall last?

Please just end this, take away my pain.
I think there is a new, but it will never be the same.

Why you? Why me?
I need help, God save me!

Take me away, cut out my heart.
Hang me by the throat and let me fall apart.

You see that you made me insane.
I can't wait to say bye, to our little game.

Hi

Hi, do you stalk me?

Huh, that's freaky.

We said goodbye, don't you remember that?

It wasn't a new hi, or do you think that?

Am I in your thoughts, when you think?

Do you see spots, even though you blink?

You're driving me insane, I'm going crazy.

This isn't a game, I'm not Mr. Maisey.

I could kill you, don't you know.

I wouldn't have to touch you, I think you know.

How do you hit someone, when you will always miss?

I'm sorry if it hurts, but I am done with this.

I have gone insane, I want to die.

So this is a game, but I will never again say hi.

Bed

This bed is too big, but I bet yours is small.
Mine is empty, but yours has it all.

My bed is clean, yours might be filthy.
I sleep on my bed, and in yours you're sinking.

I love my bed, I'll bet you love yours too.

Nothing has happened in mine, I can't say the same for you.

I Was Fine

Of course, it's you, didn't we already establish this?

I didn't ask for two, this was not my wish.

I feel like I'm breathless, almost suffocating.

Every night I'm restless, the voices in my head
constantly debating.

It's over is it not, why do I still care?

My heart is not broken, it's not, it's still there.

If something is wrong it wasn't me, it's all you.

If you're caged, then I am free. I can't fix you.

Our age, our voices, our emotions all mixed.

Our actions, our sayings, our lives, can they be fixed?

It doesn't matter what you think, I'm sorry if I can't help
you.

Tears wash down the sink, crying away the issue.

I wish you had not wasted my time.

Before I met you...

I was fine.

It's Confusing

You love me, you love me not.
Is it just a feeling or an actual thought?

Please just stop, you have my heart and you know it.
I thought you would understand how scary it is to show
it.

I'm so confused as to where we put ourselves.
It's like we are cursed as if someone cast a spell.

You think I didn't notice, is that what you see?
I wish you would make loving you more easy.

But hey, easy is lame.
So here we go again, with the heartbreak game.

You

The first time only wounded me, this time I died.
Because I found out that you were not on my side.

I don't know the story, but I got the feel.
That you had betrayed me, and I tried to conceal.

I was sad, then that sadness turned to hate.
For your apologies would arrive too late.

I was willing to forgive and to forget.
Then you returned to what was not best.

I am not broken, I have come back to life.
I pulled out what was in my back, your knife.

Once again you have tried to break my heart.
Now it will be your life that shall fall apart.

I wish you good luck and a better plan. Because I can
promise you, that I will not be there. You haven't got a
chance.

Why

Why do you make this so hard?
We get so close, then we grow so far.

I thought you loved me, or at least I loved you.
Yet you make it a quiz, and none of this feels true.

We play a game that neither of us will win.
We break each other's hearts over, and over again.

I might be too young to know what love is, but I do know
that if you are sad, then there is none of it.

Go ahead, write some more about how you feel.
If it wasn't for me, no one else would see your appeal.

I gave you the idea, and now you are complying.
So why don't you write some more where you confess to
lying.

I don't know if I miss you, or if you miss me.
I wish we could just choose whether it was or was not
meant to be.

Missing

I was missing a piece of me, and I still am.
Is there a key to be, or an open hand?

All I see is a locked door.
Not a single window, at least not anymore.

I am missing something needed for growing.
How can I continue without knowing?

This room is empty, my bed is cold.
Am I to stay this way until I grow old?

I was missing a piece of me, and I still am.
So why won't you give me the key, and give me your
hand?

Madness

What causes madness? No one could say.

But would you like it? Would you want to play?

Trapped in thoughts that scare you alone.
An eternal ringing from your brain's telephone.

Best be careful and try not to act.
But we're all a little mad, so sharpen your ax.

Tonight we fly, tonight we sing.
I'll steal you gold for a diamond ring.

Is there anyone out there that wants my heart.
Please tell me, it's tearing me apart.

Mad people are either sad, scared, angry, or stressed.
But you can also be crazy with love, oh yes.

You drive yourself crazy with your own wants.
This is what causes madness, love that taunts.

None of this is ok.

So if you ask what causes madness, what did I just say?

Cut

You can hear your voice.

The sound of it can ease your ears.
However, when you cry, you feel the silk touch of salty
tears.

To be cut and make an open wound.
To be locked away in a silent tomb.

The angels in your state of mind will guide you through
the obstacles of life.
Still, you fall to the end of the enemy's knife.

To have your soul pierced by a silver blade.
Call upon your fiery wings, and ascend into your resting
grave.

Day Nightmare

You've heard of daydreams, right?
The dreams you get but not at night.

You make them yourself with total ease.
So have you ever had ones that are not like a dream?

You feel scared for no reason.
You start to shake like it's the cold season.

The hairs on your neck stand straight.
These are the things you will get during the day.

This is what you get during a day nightmare.

These are what make the day seem like a day in a
slaughterhouse.

You start to see strange people staring at you.
You feel someone underneath grabbing your shoe.

You hear people laughing when no one is there.
This is what makes you scared.

They follow you, they see you, they talk to you.

No matter what you must pay no attention to them.

Don't look, don't peak.
If they talk to you, do not speak.

We all have day nightmares, you aren't alone.
They live with us too, we are their home.

They feed off of our fear, so please don't be afraid.
Don't cry, just listen to what I have to say.
They are reading this with you, they follow with your eyes.

You must not turn around just ignore them.

They can't hurt others, so hello day nightmare.

Our Chains

I walk with chains on my wrists.

You can't see them, but I know they are there.
Most people don't know they have them too, but if they did
they wouldn't care.

The chains lead into the pocket on my side.
The chains are made up of anger, sadness, fear, and lies.

Every time I type in what I want, the chains get tighter.
I am stuck in a dark lot. It's covered in gasoline, and I have
a lighter.

The left side of my head says, "Just get it over with".
My right side says, "Please keep looking there is still
hope."
Meanwhile, my heart says I can't trust both.

You could sell your body; you could sell your soul.
You can give away everything you have that's gold.

You can beg, you can cry.
In your head, you will hate being alive.

It's a daily struggle not to feel hurt.
So for now, I will continue on my search.

The hunt continues for someone smart with a spirit that's healthy.
I will look until I find someone who can free me from this hell that holds me.

Him

Down a dark hole, deep within the ground.
Lies the hidden home that has no sound.

You can chant as loud as you can.
You could bleed then even dance.

Still, no matter what, he won't come.

You could bathe in your blood, you could even beg.
You still won't get a nightmare when you go to bed.

You cry, you yell, and you fall, you ache.
Yet he still won't take your pain.

Go ahead and try if you will.
Die from the air or overdose on pills.

No one knows what will come after death. You might just
be gone.
However, everything you've done is lost.

I want to fly, and I want to feast.
I feel as if I am the beast.

Nobody cares, not even he.
So I still wonder what lies down beneath.

I'll always want and will always cry.
Yet for the day we meet is for another time.

Rest

The sun has come, another morning, another day.
A time in which I struggle to awake.

The dreams of the night before are fading from my mind.
Hoping I had dreamt of better times.

The reflection in the mirror is no longer what I wish to see.
I hope to look again and see someone other than me.

The clothes I wear are designed to fix my figure and shape.
So much natural beauty that has gone to waste.

Memories of the happier days are now farther than wanted.
Now only the bad ones have me haunted.

I wear a smile as a mask for the pain.
For me it's misery, for you, it's the same.

All the cruel words and rumors that spread.
Constantly filling my heart with dread.

The people who feed off of the flaws of your past and sell
it like gold.
The people who take purity away from your soul.

The love you searched for and prayed for at night.
No longer is there someone to hold you tight.

As your life deteriorates and your mind corrupts.
There is no longer you and me, and there is no longer us.

The good people who want good for life.
Their power is taken; they are deprived of their light.

What causes cruelty, what causes hate?
If it were a choice, we'd choose a different fate.

The sun is gone, the night grows near.
The darkness now brings comfort instead of fear.

The day has dragged on, so please allow me to rest.
How on earth did I survive this daily Hellfest?

The people who left me, the people who harm.
The people who make me never have open arms.

I'll sleep now, and dream away.
Dream of freedom and dream of a better day.

Forgive me, my parents, for making you scared of my death.
I don't know If I will awake, so just let me rest.

What Love Is

I miss the way my heart would beat in sync to the tunes.
I miss hearing the words I love you.

I miss sleeping to the sound of another's voice.
I miss choosing to stay by choice.

I guess some things can never really last.
I understand what happens can turn into the past.

I'm tired of staying up for hours late at night.
I'm tired of waiting in bed until I finally cry.

I'm tired of feeling nothing but all this pain.
I'm tired of nothing ever staying the same.

I don't want to be all alone.
I don't want to spend all my nights at home.

I don't want to dream of my next kiss.
I just want to know what love is.

Very Best

I had a dream the other night that I failed to do my best.
I made a bad grade because I was honest and didn't cheat on
the test.

I want to do good and reach for the stars.
Yet of course obstacles have to make it hard.

I'm not smart, brilliant, or bright.
The fear of being a failure keeps me up at night.

I'm supposed to only take one melatonin, now I take two.
I bet you would understand if it happened to you.

Hours of work that I can't understand.
Writer's block, stupidity, a curse to man.

Take a deep breath, and it'll be ok.
You don't always have to have a perfect day.

So maybe things aren't going well or great.
That doesn't mean that giving up should be your fate.

So stand up and rise above the stress.
I know that you can be the very best.

Reflection

Smile, wave, make a silly face.
Look into the reflection of your face.

Remember a time when you could just stare and be
satisfied.
How could we have known we'd lose that to others lies.

Now that image isn't how we want it to be.
The bags under your eyes are too dark. You look like you
went a week without sleep.

Has your forehead always looked so big?
Is it a condition? Do you have something that makes you
sick?

Is that a birthmark on your cheek?
It looks like a stain you'd find on bedsheets.

Has that nose been crooked all this time?
What is wrong with me? How was I confident to go
outside?

What happened to the you that you saw behind the glass.
Was it age, illness, or magic that blurred your past?

You don't want to make a silly face. It makes you look
worse.

You're an ugly disgrace!

Wait...

Stop listening to that voice in your head.
It doesn't matter what you look like in the end.

Have you noticed how your eyes catch the light?
Or how your smile shines so bright?

Your skin may not be clear, but that color is something that makes people come near.
Beauty is more than an image.

It's more than what we all see.
More than anything, it comes from within and underneath.

If you took a moment to realize what's inside your soul.
You would feel warmth instead of the cold.

You are beautiful. You are a treasure.
Smile and go look at yourself. Tell me you don't look better.

I Don't Wanna

I'm tired of being odd. I'm done with being lost.
I wish it was a phase, so I can say I forgot.

Thank you mom and dad, for the love that you gave.
I just wish I didn't have to get so much hate.

They say we are stronger; they say we bend the rules.
Then how come our past isn't in the history books?

Taste the colors, sparkle sparkle shine.
Is it really to the colors that we must bind?

I remember being younger and being so confused.
If only I had known what normal things I would lose.

I lost a couple of friends, and I'm still losing them now.
Thanks a lot mom and dad for bringing us to this town.

Maybe if I grew up somewhere more open and fun.
I wouldn't be ashamed to be different from everyone.

I'm not saying hate yourself for being you.
It's just me who is struggling to face the truth.

Sometimes I wish I could change, but change is wrong.
If I say I want it, I'm playing the enemy's song.

God If you hear me please answer my prayers and give me strength.
How many more hits do I have to take?

I tried to find love from so many places.
My heart had a beat for them all, now they're just forgotten faces.

To my love, the one who said I love you too.
I hope you conquer your demons because you're not a fool.

Now I'm back to the battle, a soldier all alone.
Fighting for myself and finding my way home.

If I could have a child and continue my blood for my dad.
Or just go back in time to warn him to be careful of which child he would have.

What's it like to be normal?

It's not like I ever knew.
So tell me, what's so bad about being you?

You don't have to face a crowd that wants you dead.
You don't have people's words ringing in your head.

Your voice isn't too high, and you don't walk with a spring.
To them, you're a person, for me, I'm a thing.

I'm a riddle, a joke.
Sorry for interrupting you when you spoke.

Tell me It's a choice, go ahead and change my mind.

I didn't choose or ask for this, so stop wasting your time.

I guess I have to put up with it. I'll go on a little longer.
Like they say, "what doesn't kill you makes you stronger."

I don't wanna be different, I don't wanna be a freak.
I don't wanna be an outcast, or be told not to speak.

It's the world that we live in, and the world that I face.
So tell me, do you really think you'd survive in my place?

It Happened

Be happy it happened, don't be sad it's over.
Even though we miss leaning on each other's shoulder.

Separated too early when we felt the bond.
We might be far apart, but we aren't gone.

One day we'll reunite and dance the night away.
We won't leave again. We'll be able to stay.

So forget about the goodbyes and remember the hellos and
the hi's.
We're truly gone if we leave each other's side.

This isn't the end of the book. It's only a chapter.
As long as we live on, that's all that matters.

Whether in a year or ten or when we are old.
Remember each smile and warm hold.

Don't be sad that it's over, be happy that it happened.

Better Now

Yeah, I'm ok. It's just a scratch like every day.

No, I'm fine. It didn't hurt all the time.

So another failed attempt hit me right in the face.
It doesn't matter now, and it won't put me in another place.

I'll walk it out or sing it loud.
Can you hear me now?

I'm tired of hearing excuses, so stop wasting my time.
I'm not tying nooses, just let me live my life.

Go ahead and cut me out, put me six feet in the ground.
I'm tired, but I'm better now.

Finding Yourself

Open the first door you see. What's behind it is always going to be something new.
When you unlock the unknown, you are free. The world has endless things to do.

Despite all the evil and cruel people of today. You are given a gift. That gift was today.
You woke up this morning in your bed, not a raft in the ocean sailing adrift.

Tell yourself that you are beautiful, and don't tell me I'm wrong. Find your happiness and live life like a love song.

Make it through the rough, and you can do great! The future depends on your action.
All of the opportunities run on fate. So if you're bored or unhappy, find a great distraction.

Finding yourself is as easy as one, two, three.
After you find yourself, you realize there is so much more.

I know you can do it. Believe in me.
As I said, it's simple, so go open that door.

My Mask

I love acting. I like to pretend.

It's easy to become another person if you have the dedication.

I like to smile. It has no end.

Happiness is not giving into temptation.

As I said before, I love acting, and I'm good at it too.

If you haven't noticed, I've always been fooling you.

Trigger

It's easy to pull someone's trigger. It's easy to unlock their full potential and vigor.

It's amazing how easy someone's life can change.
You follow a routine, but it won't always stay the same.

Finding love and sharing your heart, but then again, it is easy to fall apart.

You say you're lonely and in sorrow.
That you can barely walk and won't make it to tomorrow.

Can I just say that I am tired of being sad and listening to everyone's troubles?
Just remind yourself that things could be worse, so step out of your bubble.

You're angry because your students like to talk.
Well, there are kids in the hospital who can't even walk.

There are people who would love to be with us right now and have what you have.
Yet you only focus on yourself, and the world will always make you mad.

Newsflash, the world doesn't revolve around you. People's priorities won't always be yours.

So what if your student talks in class? Maybe tomorrow they won't return home after they walk out of their door.

So what if there is a group that is better than yours.
You are in that group because they love you. Their love is yours.

For once, can you focus on fun and love?
Just shut up and stop yelling at them, enough!

You might be lonely and hurt, but as I said, there will always be someone who has it worse.

People like to twist the words I say. They mix whatever they take.
I always have to apologize. I was even told to be fake!

Well, I say I'm done taking hits, and I'm done listening to fools.
You were once like us, so don't treat us like tools.

Everyone can change if they need to.
Ever wonder that some of your students talk in class because none of them like you?

Or maybe you don't like kids, if so, why do you work in a school?
Well, guess what, kids don't like you, so just pack your stuff and go!

PDA is not a major crime, and it is not too much.
So what if someone hugs another? Just think that you yelled at a kid after they gave their very last hug.

If it was their friend, their sibling, or cousin of blood.
You just like to bully, push around, and pick on us.

This isn't a rant on adults or any specific people.
I just want to remind you that if someone is breathing they
are people.

One day your trainee will train another.
When you're six feet in the ground they might have their
significant other.

Think about how you treat others now and ask if that's how
you want to be remembered.
Think about who would want to go to your funeral. Some
or maybe none altogether.

Just know that your actions can affect someone's hour.
That one hour could be another brick in someone's terrible
day, then they begin no power.

You keep giving those bricks and you add to those terrible
days.
That poor person, that poor kid just starts to fade.

Remember you aren't an animal, so stop acting like one.
Forget being strict, open up, spread love and have fun!

Remember every act you do is a choice, and they get
bigger and bigger.

So please be nice and kind!
Don't give that person another reason to pull that trigger.

The Mental Torture

Have you ever wanted something so bad, but have it out of reach?
Take for example a baby turtle wanting to leave its home beach.

Or have you ever had a dream that felt too far out of sight?
Never being able to grab it, the thought keeping you up at night.

I don't have my license and yes I'm an 18-year-old grad.
My excuse is that I just can't drive with the parents I have.

Mother over explains, and father makes me panic.
It's a miracle that driving doesn't make me manic.

Not only that, but I am currently unemployed.
I am just a sad excuse of a boy.

Notice how I say boy and not a man.
That is because there are too many requirements at hand.

A man must make a living, a man must fend for himself.
A man must find a way to survive with money and good health.

I have no money, and my health has always been twisted.
For being a man I check hardly any of the boxes listed.

It's not that I don't want to, or have no drive.
It's just that the world chooses to not let me feel alive.

What I want is questioned, what I feel is ignored.
My dreams have been laughed at, or make others bored.

I want to start living but how can I without transportation?
It's not like I could live off of my imagination.

I have always been too busy to get a head start like most.
I envy those who were able to act on what they chose.

I didn't choose to be stuck, I didn't choose to be late.
All I have ever asked was to free my fate.

The mental torture of not being able to do anything kills me slowly.
I might as well be the skeleton in the closet without it really showing.

I want to face reality, but I never could without a kick to the face.
Not this time however, I am taking my place.

This world is tiring, troubling, and living is hard.
Oh but how I wish I could finally start.

Needed Change

The place that I call home isn't truly mine.
It's a place where I'd hate to waste my time.

I wasn't meant to withstand the heat that this desert land
brings.
I wasn't meant for the stereotyped life that came with being
birthed here.

Never once did this town make my heart flutter and sing.
Never once did this town encourage me to cheer.

I am not the child meant to come from my parents seed.
The child they birthed was the exact opposite of what
they'd need.

I don't like what they like, I love what they hate.
I spit out what they eat, I frown at their opinions.

Oh how I wish to be given a different fate.
To rule my dominion.

I dreamt of sparkles, not dirt.
I asked for encouragement, not to get hurt.

Life has been a struggle, here in this so-called safety place.
However, soon one day I will never again have to see its
face.

I can forget the heat, the dirt, and the rain.
Instead I could finally look forward to that so needed change.

Say My Name

Say my name, just a normal name to you all. Not back home.
Say my name, what does it mean? I'm here, but back there I'm alone.

Let me tell you my story, It goes like this.
A little boy born in Texas, but there's a twist.

He grew up in his grandmother's house because his family struggled.
It took them 10 years to get money for a rental.

In that house he got his dogs and he went to middle school.
He never did wrong and followed every rule.

Now comes the twist, he doesn't know it but yeah he's gay.
It seemed that everyone knew, but not him in some way.

He was bullied, mocked, and teased.
He was called gross, weirdo, a freak.

It got worse and worse, then slightly got better.
It wasn't until long he was completely alone altogether.

He finally moved into his so-called home, a place to stay.
It didn't cross his mind, but his parents found out he was gay.

The word of it was out but not too much.
Freshman year he came out and told everyone such.

Everything turned out great, it was like a dream.
But nobody warned him that kids could be so mean.

Say my name, what does it tell you?

I wouldn't say if I had just met you.

Back home that name means many things.
Some good, some bad, I'm not a king.

Yet when I met my first crush I thought I was finally growing.
Then I realized what others saw, what I was showing.

I didn't think I was ugly, until I saw the pictures.
I was hunched over, my cheeks were puffed, I was a mixture.

Just having someone treat you in a way that talks to you without words.

You're fat, you're ugly, you're gross. That is what hurt.

So I tried and I prayed, I even changed my clothes.
I paid so much attention to the persona I showed.

I used a back brace, I would pop my neck and back.
I didn't want to continue looking like a hunchback.

Wow, you look great! I didn't know it was you at first glance.
Where's your glasses? Is that a new hairstyle? Glad to see you gave "new" a chance.

Even if I was redone and fixed up.
Still, as the years went by, I still wasn't enough.

I lost 15 pounds and always sucked in my stomach when I moved.
I constantly lost and gained as I grew.

I was borderline diabetic, I was always getting sick.
I kept asking God why my body was doing this.

I don't have abs, and I won't for some time.
Yet even if I was skinny, they say I'm not worth a try.

I was called a last resort, a last option or choice.
I couldn't measure up to the other boys.

Your voice is too high, you're too small to be a man.
I tried so hard but was never given a chance.
You say I'm your friend, you say I'm your pal.
Then why was I home alone when you all hit the town.

Do you know how painful it was to see your posts and snaps.
"Here with my best friends, here with the fam," where was my invitation to that?

Every day I had to see how much fun they all had when I wasn't there.

I always gave them presents, homemade chocolate, I always cared.

I was called too nice, so they just stepped on my heart.

Life was cruel.

Life was hard.

Then the election for theater officers came, the one they promised me.

House manager, secretary, treasurer, historian, parliamentarian, vice pres,...... president.

Four years of hard work, and only because everyone didn't like me, I got nothing.

Outcasted, outlasted, misguided, mistreated, misled.
My heart was shattered, I was broken. Alive yet somehow dead.

"Mom, I want to be homeschooled."
"Son, you make me worry."

"Dad, why are kids so cruel?"
"I don't know son, I'm sorry."

It wasn't real until I went home that night, my mom immediately began to cry.
My parents were holding hands tight.

In the car we talked about the little things, the stuff that wasn't painful to speak.
Then we went into the house, but my dad had stopped me.

He said; "Son, please be honest to us, don't lie."
"Did you ever plan, or try to commit suicide?"

Yes, Yes I did. Too many times to say.
"I try so hard mom and dad, I don't know why they treat me that way."

They sent me to counseling, I went for a few days.
It healed me a bit, but the pain will always stay.

I know I'm not perfect, but that's ok.
I will never let anyone experience my kind of pain.

I have good intentions, and so much ambition and pride.
Everyone has a purpose, so I'm going to find mine.

When I go home, I will have new hope.
Thank you all for the support when I needed it the most.

I don't care if I'm nothing, I don't care if I don't fit in.

I have the memories and new strength from within.

Thank you all again, I love you all the same.
So I don't care about what way anyone from home will say my name.

Grandma

My angel, my light. My sender of love every night.
You are my strength, you are my faith. You are my protector
from anger and hate.

Although I couldn't always hold your hand when you were
scared.
I hope that it comforted you to know that I cared.

My heart will never forget the impact you gave.
For it was your love that kept me safe.

I promised God, that I would be good as long as you were
by my side.
I know that you will always be there to hold me tight.

I will make you proud and I will always try.
There will never be a reason for me to say goodbye.

You have always been the one to love me for me.
Through sadness and pain, to my hope you have the key.

Life isn't always fair, and it never will be.
But I can sleep a little easier knowing you will always be
with me.

In spirit, in faith, and always with love.

Forever and always when the day comes that you are up above.

Your best act was helping me realize how precious time is. The past is history, but the present is a gift.

So now the time that I read this to you is the best I have. I'll put my faith into God and thank him for what we had.

My angel, my light. My sender of love every night.

Thank you. I love you.

Meet Evrin

The picture above is Evrin at age 18, when he finished this book. Evrin always had a passion for writing. When we turned 12 years old he realized that he could channel his emotions into his words. Every time his heart was broken, or felt like he couldn't go on, he wrote a poem about how he felt.

He hopes to create more books of poetry and to inspire others in many ways.

www.worksbyevrin.com